THINGS WE EAT

THINGS
WE
EAT

by

Sylvia Vardell & Janet Wong

Pomelo
Books

**100% of the profits from this book
will be donated
to the IBBY Children in Crisis Fund**

IBBY CHILDREN IN CRISIS

The IBBY Children in Crisis Fund provides support for children whose lives have been disrupted through war, civil disorder, or natural disaster. The program gives immediate support and help – and also aims for long-term community impact, aligning with IBBY's goal of giving every child the right to become a reader.

ibby.org/awards-activities/ibby-children-in-crisis-fund
usbby.org/donate.html

Pomelo Books
4580 Province Line Road
Princeton, NJ 08540
PomeloBooks.com
info@pomelobooks.com

Library of Congress Cataloging-in-Publication Data is available.

ISBN 978-1-937057-31-2

Please visit us:
PomeloBooks.com

POEMS BY

Gail Aldous	George Ella Lyon
Rebecca Balcárcel	JoAnn Early Macken
David Bowles	Elisabeth Norton
Sandy Brehl	Lisa Varchol Perron
Carol Bullman	Jama Kim Rattigan
Yangsook Choi	Joan Riordan
Kelly Conroy	Pamela Ross
Nicola Davies	Donna JT Smith
Rebecca Kai Dotlich	April Halprin Wayland
Linda A. Dryfhout	Vicki Wilke
Theresa Gaughan	Janet Wong
Mary Lee Hahn	Jacqueline Woodson
Georgia Heard	Sarah Ziman

TABLE OF CONTENTS

A

AVOCADO

by Kelly Conroy

Look at me!
I'm in a tree
testing my bravado.
I'm climbing high,
up to the sky
to reach that avocado.

I'll pluck it,
   cut it,
      gut it, then
I'll sprinkle it with lime.
And when my snack is gone
I'll pick –
another tree to climb.

B

BAGEL

by Pamela Ross

Chew and bite into soft dough
Munch it fast or munch it slow

Top it, schmear it, lox or cheese
Or keep it plain, if you please

I peek at you and let you see
How good a bagel tastes to me!

COOKIE

by Jama Kim Rattigan

Who ate the last cookie?
I really cannot say.
Was it chunky chewy chocolate chip,
baked fresh today?

Crumbs are on my face? How odd.
Haven't got a clue.
If I find the missing cookie,
I'll eat it just for you.

14

DUMPLING

by Yangsook Choi

Meat minced
Onion diced
Tofu squashed
Cabbage sliced

Filling spooned
Dumpling formed . . .
Mouth delighted
Heart warmed

E

EGG

by Vicki Wilke

My Papa raises chickens.
I named one Mary Lou.
She scratches and she pecks,
Like chickens always do.

We have our conversations –
And we never disagree.
I thank her for each lovely egg.
She buk-buks back at me.

F

FISH

by Carol Bullman

I'm fishin' and wishin' for dinner –
Just dreamin' with Dad by the lake.
A tug on the line . . .
This fish will be mine!
But wait! There has been some mistake!

This fish has red eyes that are googly.
It's floppy and scaly and slick.
Set this one free!
The right fish for me
Comes fried and is shaped like a stick!

G

GRAPE

by Sandy Brehl

Juicy bulb with dewy skin?

GRAPE!

Drips of sunlight down your chin?

GRAPE!

Luscious, scrumptious, sweet-tart bite?

GRAPE!

Grapes are mouthfuls of delight!

H

HAMBURGER

by JoAnn Early Macken

What burger? Hamburger,
nutburger, yamburger,
mushroom-and-beanburger,
biggest-you've-seen burger.
Burger with pickles
and onions and cheese,
ketchup and mustard
and lettuce? Yes, please!

ICING

by Joan Riordan

Icing on cupcakes.
Icing on hearts.
Icing on cookies.
Icing on tarts.
Icing on fingers,
elbows and wrists.
I sing while icing –
in ribbons and twists!

J

JAM

by Donna JT Smith

Huckleberry,
  raspberry,
    pick them off the vine.
Elderberry,
  strawberry,
    juicy, ripe and fine!
Boysenberry,
  blueberry,
    lovely in a pie
But –
all the berries
  (and cherries)
    make a jam divine!

K

KIMCHI

by Janet Wong

This **kimchi** might be cold
but it's really spicy hot,
so I dip a piece in water
and I wash the pepper off.
It tastes SO good I cannot stop . . .
I eat it with dumplings
and tofu and rice.
And after ten bites
I don't even mind the spice.
Now I eat it without rinsing,
with fish and meat.

Kimchi on the table
makes our dinner complete!

L

LETTUCE

by Mary Lee Hahn

Lettuce tastes like sunshine.
Every leaf is flavored
with clouds and wind and rain,
as crisp and cool as early morning.

M

MANGO

by Rebecca Balcárcel

The mango trees know magic spells
that grow my favorite fruit.
Sparkles of sun become sweetness.
Water and raindrops make juice.

When rich soil mixes with time,
when bird song and breezes are spun,
mangos will ripen for eating.
First bite – a zing on my tongue!

NUT

by George Ella Lyon

A peanut
is not a tree nut.
It does not grow
on a tree.
Peanuts
grow in neat pods
like green beans
and peas.

But they don't grow
on vines. No!
They grow
underground.
Down with the roots
that's where
peanuts
are found.

ORANGE

by Lisa Varchol Perron

You picked me! At last,
I have somewhere to go.
Life in this market
is dreadfully slow.

Your mother says oranges
aren't on her list.
But *I* am an orange
too sweet to resist!

PIZZA

by Rebecca Kai Dotlich

Together we cheer
Game on! Pizza's here . . .

so bring on the laughs
and a round of hoorays:
we're in for good times
in all kinds of ways.

We give out high-fives
as we shout out the score.
We each grab a piece,
then one or two more.

Game over! Score tight.
Pizza for the win tonight.

QUICHE

by Gail Aldous

Whisk eggs,
add cream,
ham,
spinach,
and cheese.
Mix. Pour
in crust.
Bake. Wait.
Cool.
Bite, eat.
QUICHE!

R

RICE

by Jacqueline Woodson

I think my favorite food
no matter what my mood
is rice.
A globe inside a bowl
is tasty hot or cold
but a pile upon a plate
is also great.
With veggies, meat, or plain
I always eat every grain.

S

SOUP

by Georgia Heard

It's time for soup,
let's eat some soup,
with beans and rice
and broth (one scoop).
Dip the ladle in the pot
serve it steaming, piping hot.
It's time for soup,
let's eat some soup.
Soup, soup
delicious soup!

T
OPEN
MOTOWN
TACOS
TACOS
TACOS
GREAT
TIMES GREAT FOOD
TACO

TACO

by April Halprin Wayland

Every Friday smells like tacos.
Paco's truck parks on our street.

Friday's Día de los Tacos.
Me and Mama come to eat!

Every Friday's warm tortillas
filled with salsa, cheese, and meat.

Paco winks, spoons extra guac –
avocado-yummy treat!

U

UDON

by Sarah Ziman

If you don't know udon,
That's something to undo.
They're soft and hot and slippery –
The best noodles to chew!

Catch them with your chopsticks
And slurp them up real fast.
The hardest thing with udon
Is making udon last!

V

VEGETABLE

by Nicola Davies

Between the rows
I put my foot on the soft, soft earth.

Between the rows
I felt the shade cool my skin.

Between the rows
I saw beetles walk and worms wiggle.

Between the rows I heard a robin sing.
Between the rows I was quiet and careful.

Look at all the vegetables I picked,
between the rows!

W

WAFFLE

by Theresa Gaughan

Daddy helped me make it.
He told me what to do.
I measured the flour, cracked the eggs,
and stirred the milk in, too.

A waffle with berries and honey
is my favorite weekend treat.
I made it with my daddy,
and now it's time to eat!

XOCOLATL

by David Bowles

Abuela showed my cousin and me
how to make chocolatey cocoa treats.
She also taught us the native names
used by our ancestors – and nowadays.

The word cacao is Mayan, wow!
And xocolatl comes from Nahuatl.
It's a bean we like to eat a lot of
and sip as syrup from the bottle!

Y

YOGURT

by Elisabeth Norton

A rainbow of yogurt.
Which one shall I choose?
Each color's a flavor –
Red, yellow and blue.
Banana and strawberry,
Lemon and peach.
All creamy and yummy –
I'll take one of each!

Z

ZUCCHINI

by Linda A. Dryfhout

A B C D E F G

H I J K

L M N O P

Q R S T U V

W X Y Z

ALPHABET MENU

by Janet Wong

The restaurant takeout menu
shows the foods that we can get.
"You can read?" the waiter asks.
I say, "I know the alphabet!"

Combo A is spicy chicken.
Combo B is soup with fish.
I say, "C, please! Curry rice
is my all-time favorite dish."

"Combo B," the waiter says,
and writes it down in a hurry.
"No, not B. That is wrong, sir.
Combo C," I say, "like CURRY!"

RESOURCES FOR PARENTS & TEACHERS

TIPS FOR READERS

Here are some basic strategies for sharing poetry with children. Whether you're a family member, caregiver, teacher, librarian, or school administrator, these tips will help you get kids excited about reading!

Reading the pictures
With very young children, reading begins with everything EXCEPT the words. Encourage children to "read" or interpret the pictures and talk about what they see. Which foods can they name and identify? Invite them to talk about their own cooking or gardening or grocery shopping experiences.

Reading aloud
Even if your child can read independently, it's good to hear poems read aloud for their sound qualities. Poems are meant to be read out loud to savor the words, sounds, and rhythm. Plus reading aloud together is a bonding time that makes reading a positive experience for young children just beginning to master the skills of reading.

Props and pantomime
Whether you're reading to a group of children or just one child, simple props or pantomime can make your read-aloud come alive. If you have it handy, use a food depicted in the poem as a "poetry prop," and hold it up while reading aloud. Or use gestures such as stirring ingredients in a bowl when reading the poems *Quiche* or *Waffle* or casting a fishing rod while reading *Fish*.

Combine listening and reading with echo reading
With echo reading, a child or a group of children will repeat lines of a poem after hearing you read them. Pause after each line and put a hand to your ear to cue your readers to repeat what they've just heard.

Point to words

Pointing to words as you read them is a great way to help children learn to read and helps them begin to associate the spoken word with the written word. It also reinforces the concept that English text moves from left to right, top to bottom.

Encourage guessing

Children often like rhyming poems because it's easy to guess the words that come at regular rhyming intervals. They sometimes will guess the wrong words, but it's good to encourage guessing; it makes reading feel like a game and builds prediction skills essential to comprehension.

Read parts

Some poems have a repeated word or phrase that you can point out before you start reading. You can read just the line with those repeated words before you read the whole poem. You don't need to read the whole poem each time!

Read, respond, and be open

Sometimes you'll want to talk to children to hear their reactions to a poem, but it's also fine just to read a poem and move on. If you do pause to chat, be open to their responses; children often notice surprising things and make unusual connections.

Record the reading

Record a poem to share with a friend or family member far away. It's easy to make an audio or video recording of a child reading either alone or together with you using your phone or an online tool such as Zoom or Google Meet. Or record yourself reading for your child to enjoy later when you may be away.

FUN ACTIVITIES TO TRY

Here are some activities for having fun with poetry in more creative ways after you've read and shared each poem.

Poem titles
Each poem has a one-word title and that word also appears in the poem itself in a different color. This makes it easy for children to join in on that key word as you read the rest of the poem aloud and point to the word when it's their turn.

Learning letters
After reading the poem aloud, challenge children to think of other words that start with the same initial letter. For example, for A = *Avocado*, you might offer *apple, alligator, art*, etc. Can you work together to think of other words that rhyme with the poem title word? For example, in F = *Fish*, the word rhymes with *wish* or *dish* and so on.

Action
Several poems in this book use action or movement to help children engage in the poem. For example, encourage children to pantomime tree climbing while you read *Avocado*, giving high fives in *Pizza*, or mixing imaginary ingredients in a bowl while you share *Waffle* or *Quiche*.

Time for poetry
Reading a poem out loud takes less than a minute! Add a quick poem to your routine to build incidental literacy development. Start the day with a poem at breakfast, copy and add a food poem to a lunch bag, or end the day with a poem read at dinner or at bedtime. Commemorate the first day of school with a poem, or the last day of school, or "moving up" day. You can also share a poem to celebrate a birthday.

Translate

Translate your favorite poem into another language spoken in your family or community. You can work with a friend or a neighbor or try GoogleTranslate to see how your poem sounds in French or Chinese or another language.

Poems in parts

Several poems in this book use italics (or quotation marks or all capital letters) for key words or phrases, which provides a helpful cue for reading a poem in parts. You can read most of the poem and then cue children to read the word or phrase in italics, quotes, or capitals. Try this approach with the poems *Pizza, Quiche,* or *Grape*.

Foods

All of the poems in this book are about a specific food. As you share each poem, talk with children about the origins of that food: where is it found, grown, made, or purchased? Invite children to talk about new foods they have tried or about their favorite foods.

Family poems

Several poems are about moments we share with our families. Work with children to share *Egg* or *Fish* or *Taco* or *Waffle* with parents and caregivers. Talk about what foods their own families enjoy.

Types of poems

There are several different types of poems in this book, some rhyming like *Nut* or *Yogurt* and some free verse or non-rhyming like *Lettuce* or *Vegetable*. Some have just a little bit of rhyme, like *Quiche*. Some are "list" poems like *Hamburger* and *Jam*. Children may enjoy writing their own list poems about foods they like.

WEB RESOURCES

There are so many useful literacy resources online that it's sometimes hard to know where to start. You'll find basic information and engaging activities at the following recommended websites. Dive in and have fun!

nutrition.gov
Here you'll find helpful information on nutrition, healthy eating, physical activity, tasty recipes, and food safety with a special "kids' corner."

kidsgardening.org
This site provides information for educators and caregivers about the value of gardening in helping kids engage their natural curiosity and wonder. They offer grants, contests, programs, and resources.

everychildareader.net
Every Child a Reader connects book creators with learning communities, providing literacy tools and resources. Their many outreach programs include the Kids' Book Choice Awards.

ibby.org
The International Board on Books for Young People (IBBY) is an international network with dozens of chapters all over the world working together to connect children with books.

kidlit.tv
KidLit TV creates videos that highlight brand new books and the authors and illustrators who created them. They also offer arts and crafts activities and live coverage of special literary events.

naeyc.org
The National Association for the Education of Young Children (NAEYC) is
a membership organization that provides professional development and
support for early childhood educators and families.

nokidhungry.org
No Kid Hungry is the only national campaign focused on ending childhood
hunger in the U.S. and works to help schools, state agencies, and non-
profit groups with policy information, research reports, grants, and other
resources.

reachoutandread.org
Endorsed by the American Academy of Pediatrics (AAP), this site provides
early literacy tools in Spanish, screen-free activities, and links to even
more resources for reading with children.

readingrockets.org
Reading Rockets is an education initiative of the public television station
WETA. In their "Reading Topics A-Z" you can find online resources on
autism, dyslexia, and much more.

usbby.org
The United States Board on Books for Young People (USBBY) is the U.S.
national section of IBBY, with an Outstanding International Books List that
features titles for children that promote global understanding.

WNDB: diversebooks.org
We Need Diverse Books (WNDB) is a grassroots organization with
resources on race, equity, anti-racism, and inclusion. Their mission is
putting more books with diverse characters into the hands of all children.

ABOUT THE POETS

You probably found some favorite poems when reading this book. Write down the poets' names and learn more about them by visiting their websites and blogs. Then look for more of their poems (and books)!

Gail Aldous   scbwi.org/members-public/gail-aldous
Gail Aldous is a former special education teacher and reading teacher who writes for children and young adults. She enjoys eating quiche with ham, spinach, and lots of cheese.

Rebecca Balcárcel   rebeccabalcarcel.com
Rebecca Balcárcel is the award-winning author of *The Other Half of Happy*, a middle-grade novel, and the poetry book *Palabras in Each Fist*. She loves mango sorbet, mango smoothies, and best of all, mangos!

David Bowles   davidbowles.us
David Bowles is the author of 27 books, including *My Two Border Towns*. It's full of his family's favorite foods, like hot Mexican chocolate. "Xocolatl" was the first Nahuatl word he learned as a teen.

Sandy Brehl   sandybrehlbooks.com
Sandy Brehl is the author of middle grade books, a picture book, and poetry in Spider Magazine. She loves working with other writers. Sharing stories and poetry is luscious and satisfying – like a juicy grape!

Carol Bullman   achildrensbookworld.com
Carol Bullman is the author of the picture books *Your Nursery Is an Everywhere* and *The Christmas House*. You're likely to catch her at water's edge daydreaming rather than fishing, but she still enjoys a good fish stick!

Yangsook Choi   yangsookchoi.com
Yangsook Choi has written and illustrated many picture books including *The Name Jar* and *New Cat*. Growing up in Korea, she enjoyed watching her grandma make gigantic dumplings for her family. Inspired by her grandma, she loves to throw a dumpling-making party.

Kelly Conroy   kellyconroy.com
Kelly Conroy is a picture book writer, poet, and former actuary who loves all things magical, whimsical, and numerical. Her goal in life is to make people smile. You can find her eating avocado toast in Pennsylvania or dreaming about avocado trees in Hawaii.

Nicola Davies   nicola-davies.com
Nicola Davies is the author of more than 80 books including the eco-adventure novel *The Song That Sings Us* and *Many,* a picture book about biodiversity. She likes spending time in her garden and growing vegetables to eat.

Rebecca Kai Dotlich   rebeccakaidotlich.com
Rebecca Kai Dotlich writes poems about everything from mud to marbles; one of her latest books is *The Knowing Book*. Growing up, she feels certain she made over one million pizzas to eat with her older brother while they watched "The Twilight Zone."

Linda A. Dryfhout   Twitter: @LADryfhout
Linda A. Dryfhout is a poet whose work has appeared in magazines and anthologies such as *Hop to It: Poems to Get You Moving*. She enjoys growing her own telephone-size zucchini and canning vegetables from her garden.

Theresa Gaughan   Twitter: @TheresaGaughan
Theresa Gaughan is a veteran teacher. She loves writing and sharing poetry with her third-grade students. As a weekend treat, she enjoys a buttery waffle with fresh strawberries.

Mary Lee Hahn   maryleehahn.com
Mary Lee Hahn is the author of *Reconsidering Read-Aloud* and her poems have been published in more than a dozen anthologies. She loves the many green flavors of all kinds of lettuce.

Georgia Heard   georgiaheard.com
Georgia Heard is the author of 19 books including her latest *My Thoughts Are Clouds: Poems for Mindfulness* and *Boom! Bellow! Bleat!: Animal Poems for Two or More Voices*. Her favorite soup is New England clam chowder served with oyster crackers.

George Ella Lyon   georgeellalyon.com
George Ella Lyon is the author of over 50 books, including *All the Water in the World*. She likes almond butter toast with blueberry jam for breakfast, and GORP (Good Old Raisins and Peanuts) for a snack.

JoAnn Early Macken   joannmacken.com
JoAnn Early Macken lives in Wisconsin, where she writes, walks, sews, gardens, and tries out recipes for plant-based foods. *Grow* is her newest book, and black bean-walnut is her favorite burger.

Elisabeth Norton   elisabethnorton.com
Elisabeth Norton is an English teacher and writer who loves playing with words to create poems and books for young readers. Originally from the United States, she lives with her family in Switzerland. She likes to eat coconut milk yogurt with a spoonful of honey.

Lisa Varchol Perron   lisaperronbooks.com
Lisa Varchol Perron is a children's poet and author. Her debut picture book and a rhyming board book will be released in 2023. She can't resist a sweet orange, especially in an orange-avocado salad.

Jama Kim Rattigan   jamarattigan.com
Jama Kim Rattigan is a former English teacher, children's book author, and hungry baker. She blogs at Jama's Alphabet Soup, where she's become an expert at finding and eating lost cookies.

Joan Riordan   Twitter: @JRiordan173
Joan Riordan is a teacher with decades of experience and the co-author of *Doing Language Arts in Morning Meeting*. She enjoys creating, walking, and baking. When eating cake, she always saves the icing for last.

Pamela Ross   pamelarosswrites.com
Pamela Ross is the author of nonfiction books for children and her poems have appeared in online and print anthologies. She loves going to diners to eat a warm, buttery egg bagel with a hot cup of coffee.

Donna JT Smith   mainelywrite.blogspot.com
Donna JT Smith loves writing happy poems, collecting rocks and beach glass, and picking berries to make blueberry jam. Donna also loves snuggling with her little dog, Daisy, who helps her eat that jam!

April Halprin Wayland   aprilwayland.com
April Halprin Wayland is a poet, author, and teacher. Her award-winning books include the verse novel *Girl Coming in for a Landing*, and the picture book *More Than Enough ~ a Passover Story*. Her favorite tacos? Shrimp!

Vicki Wilke   winningwriters.com/people/vicki-wilke
Vicki Wilke taught young children for 33 years, while joyfully writing and publishing poetry for adults and her students. Now retired, she still puts her pencil to paper, sleeps in, and enjoys her egg and veggie omelettes.

Jacqueline Woodson   jacquelinewoodson.com
Jacqueline Woodson is the author of a whole lot of books for young people. She has won many top awards, including the Astrid Lindgren Memorial Award (ALMA) and the Hans Christian Andersen Award. Next to pizza, rice is her favorite food.

Sarah Ziman   sarahziman.co.uk
Sarah Ziman is from beautiful Wales and has poems in various anthologies and magazines. She likes udon noodles with shrimp, garlic, and lots of chili. (Her cat only likes the shrimp part!)

POEM CREDITS

ABOUT VARDELL & WONG

Sylvia M. Vardell is Professor in the School of Library and Information Studies at Texas Woman's University and teaches graduate courses in children's and young adult literature. Vardell has published extensively, including five books on literature for children as well as over 25 book chapters and 100 journal articles. In 2020, she curated the anthology *A World Full of Poems: Inspiring Poetry for Children*. She loves her mother's German cooking, especially rouladen, red cabbage, and potato dumplings with lots of gravy. Learn more about her at SylviaVardell.com.

Janet Wong is a graduate of Yale Law School and a former lawyer. She has written more than 35 books for children on a wide variety of subjects, including chess (*Alex and the Wednesday Chess Club*) and yoga (*TWIST: Yoga Poems*). She is the 2021 winner of the NCTE Excellence in Poetry for Children Award, a lifetime achievement award that is one of the highest honors a children's poet can receive. When she was a child, she saw her mother's family make kimchi on their farm in Korea, burying large clay pots in the ground; as an adult, she now buys kimchi at the supermarket. Learn more about her at JanetWong.com.

Together, Vardell & Wong are the creative forces behind Pomelo Books.

ABOUT POMELO BOOKS

Pomelo Books is Poetry PLUS. Poetry PLUS play. Poetry PLUS science. Poetry PLUS holidays. Poetry PLUS pets — and more. We make it EASY to share poetry any time of day!

Successful K-12 teachers and administrators build regular "touch points" into their routines to create a safe and engaging learning environment. Poetry can be a powerful tool for offering a shared literary experience in just a few minutes, with both curricular benefits and emotional connections for students at all levels.

Our books in *The Poetry Friday Anthology* series and the *Poetry Friday Power Book* series make it easy to use poetry for integrating skills, building language learning, crossing curricular areas, mentoring young writers, promoting critical thinking, fostering social-emotional development, and inviting students to respond creatively.

A shared poetry moment can help build a classroom community filled with kindness, respect, and joy. Learn more at PomeloBooks.com.

OTHER BOOKS BY
VARDELL & WONG

Things We Do

A CBC Hot Off the Press selection

What things do we love to do? In this book you'll find poems from A to Z, featuring action words and photos that will make kids eager to ASK, BEND, CLAP, DANCE, EAT, FLY, GROW, HUG, INVENT, JUMP, KICK, LAUGH, MAKE, NAP, OPEN, PLAY, QUACK, READ, SIGN, TYPE, UNPACK, VISIT, WAVE, X-RAY, YAWN, and ZOOM as you read the playful poems. This poetry anthology is ideal for students in preschool through Grade 1 and can be shared by families at home or by teachers in classrooms. Parents, caregivers, and educators will find useful tips and resources to help make learning even more fun. This book will also be a favorite resource in an ELL classroom.

100% of the profits from this "THINGS WE . . . " series will be donated to the IBBY Children in Crisis Fund (IBBY.org).

Hop to It: Poems to Get You Moving

Kids' Choice Book Award "Best Book of Facts" Winner

This anthology of 100 poems by 90 poets gets kids thinking and moving as they use pantomime, sign language, and whole body movements, including deskercise! You'll also find poems on current topics, such as life during a pandemic. Take a 30-second indoor recess whenever you need it!

The Poetry Friday Anthology for Celebrations

ILA Notable Books for a Global Society

This fun book features 156 poems (in both Spanish & English) honoring a wide variety of traditional and non-traditional holidays from all over the world. (Also available in a Teacher/Librarian Edition.)

"A bubbly and educational bilingual poetry anthology for children." – Kirkus

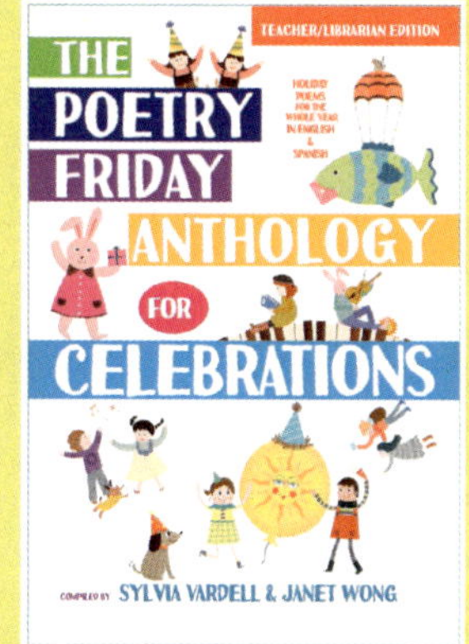

Pet Crazy: A Poetry Friday Power Book

A CBC Hot Off the Press selection

This interactive story – with Hidden Language Skills that engage kids in "playing" with punctuation, spelling, and other basics – features three characters who love spending time with animals. Extensive back matter features resources for helping young people perform, read, write, and try to publish poetry.

"An enthusiastic invitation for kids to celebrate their animal friends through poetry composition." – Kirkus

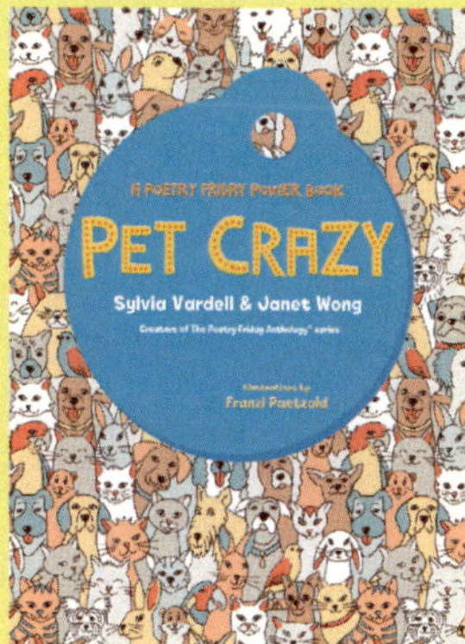

The Poetry of Science

An NSTA Recommends selection

T*he Poetry of Science* is an illustrated book for children that contains 250 poems on science, technology, engineering, and math organized by topic. (A companion Teacher/Librarian Edition features mini-lessons and resources).

"A treasury of the greatest science poetry for children ever written, with a twist." – NSTA

Made in the USA
Monee, IL
22 March 2022